Asthma

ANN O. SQUIRE

Children's Press®
An Imprint of Scholastic Inc.

Content Consultant
Karen E. Peters, DrPH
Clinical Assistant Professor
Division of Community Health Sciences
School of Public Health
University of Illinois—Chicago
Chicago, Illinois

Library of Congress Cataloging-in-Publication Data
Squire, Ann O.
 Asthma / by Ann O. Squire.
     pages cm. — (A true book)
 Includes bibliographical references and index.
 Audience: 9–12
 Audience: Grade 4 to 6
 ISBN 978-0-531-21471-8 (library binding) — ISBN 978-0-531-21521-0 (pbk.)
 1. Asthma—Juvenile literature. 2. Asthma in children—Juvenile literature. I. Title.
 RC591.S68 2016
 618.92'238—dc23   2014046958

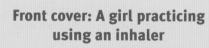

Front cover: A girl practicing using an inhaler
Back cover: An illustraton of human lungs

Find the Truth!

Everything you are about to read is true *except* for one of the sentences on this page.

Which one is **TRUE**?

T or F   There are no long-term treatments for asthma.

T or F   Asthma can develop in adults.

Find the answers in this book.

Contents

THE **BIG** TRUTH!

No smoking sign

There are a variety of medicines to help treat asthma.

Nebulizers are powered by batteries or electricity.

CHAPTER 1

What Can It Be?

It was morning recess at Harbor Elementary School. The playground was filled with children running, jumping, playing ball, and enjoying the spring weather. But not everyone was having fun. Kyle and his sister, Alyssa, had been playing kickball. Then Kyle put his hands to his chest and started panting. Alyssa led him to a bench. She stayed with him while he rested. She was worried about her brother. He wasn't looking well at all.

 For most people with asthma, exercise can trigger an attack.

Trouble Breathing

Kyle was tired, even though he hadn't been playing very hard. He took quick, shallow breaths. Each time he breathed out, or exhaled, he heard a little whistling sound. His chest felt tight, as though a band were wrapped around it. He couldn't seem to catch his breath. Even though

he had been resting on the bench for 10 minutes, he didn't feel any better. It seemed that breathing was becoming more difficult, rather than easier.

Breathing issues like Kyle's can come on suddenly and without warning.

8

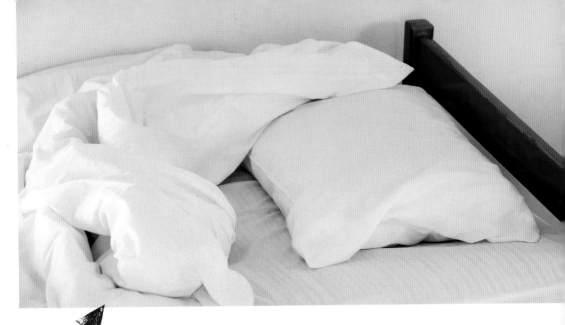

Breathing problems can worsen at night.

Kyle wondered if he was feeling so bad because of last night. He had woken up four or five times during the night, coughing and wheezing. His chest had felt tight, just as it did right now. Whenever he tried to go back to sleep, the coughing would start again. As a result, Kyle had hardly slept at all. Maybe that was why he had dark circles under his eyes and felt so sick this morning.

When a person is worried about his or her health, it is often best to ask a doctor about it.

When the kids got home from school, Kyle went straight to his bedroom to rest. Alyssa told their mom what had happened. Their mom was worried. She had heard Kyle coughing the past few nights. She also noticed he looked tired. She had assumed he had caught another spring cold. But what Alyssa described sounded more serious. While Kyle slept, his mother picked up the phone and called the doctor.

Asthma Triggers

Many different things can bring on an asthma attack. Some people are sensitive to many of the following triggers, and some to just a few.

Allergens: Pollen; mold; cockroach droppings; dust; certain foods; flakes of skin, called dander, that are shed from animals

Irritants: Perfumes, chemicals in the air, smoke, air pollution, cold air

Medicines: Aspirin or some other pain relievers

Illnesses: Colds, **infections** in the lungs or **sinuses**

Exercise: High-energy activities such as running

Stomachache: Stomach acid backs up and irritates the esophagus, which connects the stomach to the throat

Emotions: Crying, laughing, emotional upsets

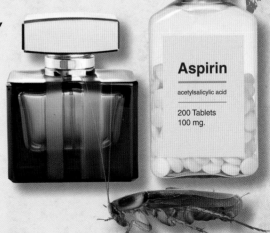

Aspirin

acetylsalicylic acid

200 Tablets
100 mg.

Making a Diagnosis

A few days later, Kyle visited the doctor. The doctor first asked about his **symptoms**, how long they had been going on, and other times he had been sick. Then she learned about Kyle's activities at school and his home life. The doctor was interested to learn that the family had recently adopted two kittens. The family had quickly discovered their dad was allergic to them.

 Cat allergies are far more common than dog allergies.

Looking for Clues

The next step was a physical exam. The doctor could hear a soft wheezing sound as Kyle breathed. He looked pale and tired and seemed out of breath. The doctor took his temperature. She used a stethoscope to listen to his lungs. She peered into his eyes, ears, and throat. Kyle didn't have a fever, body aches, or a sore throat. This told the doctor that Kyle's symptoms were not caused by a cold or the flu.

A doctor listens to his patient's lungs as she breathes.

14

Mild allergy symptoms are often limited to sneezing, coughing, a stuffy nose, or irritated skin.

Is It an Allergy?

One possibility was that Kyle had an allergy to something. The tendency to have allergies runs in families. Kyle's dad was allergic to the kittens. This made it more likely that Kyle would have an allergy as well. His allergy could be to the kittens or to another substance altogether. But Kyle had some different symptoms, such as the wheezing and the tight feeling in his chest. It seemed that something else was going on.

An asthma attack occurs when asthma symptoms worsen.

Breathing Test

The doctor suspected that Kyle might be suffering from asthma. In this disease, a person's airways are swollen and clogged with a thick, sticky liquid called **mucus**. It makes it difficult to breathe and can cause wheezing and tightness, just as Kyle was feeling. To check for asthma, the doctor used a spirometry test. The test would measure how much air was flowing in and out of Kyle's lungs.

To perform the test, the doctor placed soft clips over Kyle's nose. Then she handed him a plastic mouthpiece attached to the spirometer. He took a deep breath and exhaled as hard and fast as he could into the mouthpiece. They repeated the test a few times. Each time, the amount of air he breathed out was very low. The air was also very slow to exit his lungs. This showed that Kyle's airways were too narrow.

Nose clips prevent any air from escaping from the nose rather than the mouth. This makes the spirometry test more accurate.

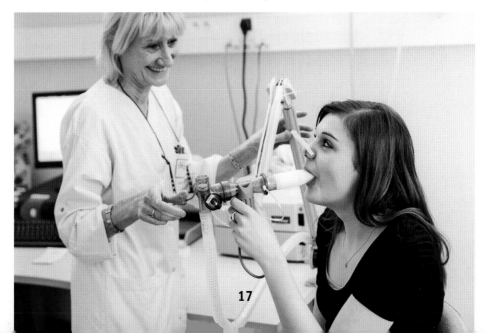

Opening the Airways

Next, the doctor had Kyle inhale, or breathe in, a medicine called a bronchodilator. It is designed to relax the muscles of the bronchial tubes, the air passages leading to the lungs. After waiting for the medicine to take effect, the doctor repeated the spirometry test. This time, the results were normal. This meant that asthma was causing Kyle's symptoms.

Rescue inhalers provide medicine that acts fast but does not last long.

An inhaler delivers bronchodilator medicine through the mouth to the lungs.

18

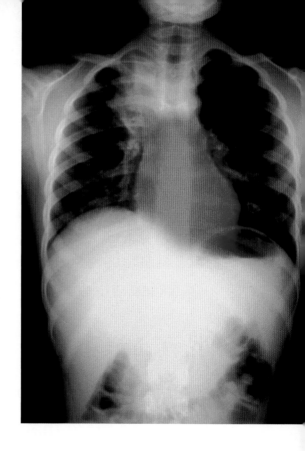

An x-ray allows a doctor to check for swelling and see if a substance is clogging up a patient's lungs.

Other Tests

Kyle's asthma was easy to diagnose. However, some patients require more tests. The doctor might suspect that symptoms are caused by exercise or cold air. Then the doctor performs the spirometry test before and after the patient experiences these triggers. She may have the patient inhale methacholine (meth-uh-KOH-leen). This substance tightens the airways in people who have asthma. The doctor might also order an x-ray of the chest or sinuses to rule out other problems.

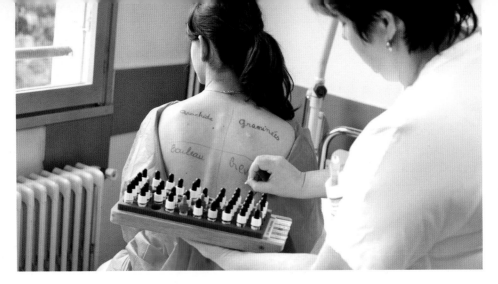

A scratch test is usually done on a patient's back or arm.

The Scratch Test

Like many people who develop asthma, Kyle had always had more than his share of colds and **respiratory** infections. Now he had asthma, and he needed a plan to control it. First, the doctor wanted to investigate Kyle's asthma triggers. Many people with asthma have allergies, and allergens often trigger asthma attacks. So the doctor performed an allergy scratch test. This would tell her whether Kyle was sensitive to certain allergens in his environment.

The doctor cleaned Kyle's skin with alcohol. Then she made tiny scratches with a needle. She placed a drop of fluid containing a different allergen onto each scratch. After about 20 minutes, Kyle's skin was red and swollen under the drop of pollen. This meant Kyle was allergic to pollen. It was no surprise his asthma symptoms flared up in the spring. Flowering trees surrounded the school playground. These flowers produced pollen, which triggered Kyle's asthma attack.

A pollen count is a measure of how much pollen is in the air.

Trees generally bloom in late winter and throughout the spring.

21

Asthma Through the Ages

Asthma is not a new disease. The Greek doctor Hippocrates (right) described asthma symptoms around 400 B.C.E. He said that they were most likely to occur among tailors, metalworkers, and fishermen. Several hundred years later, another doctor accurately described it as a blockage of the bronchial tubes. He suggested treating it with a mixture of owl's blood and wine.

As years went by, doctors learned more about asthma. One doctor working in the 1600s discovered that asthma could be worsened by dust and intense exercise.

However, in the early 20th century, many doctors believed asthma was caused by depression or other mental illnesses. It was not until the 1960s that doctors recognized that asthma is airway inflammation. Then they began treating patients with anti-inflammatory medicines. These medicines are still in use today.

About 8 percent of adults in the United States have asthma.

CHAPTER 3

What Causes Asthma?

Asthma is a disease in which a person's bronchial tubes become inflamed. This causes the airways to narrow and makes breathing difficult, as Kyle found out. Asthma is a chronic condition. This means that, in most cases, it will not go away. Even when a person is not experiencing symptoms, the disease is still there. The bronchial tubes are always more inflamed than those of a person who does not have asthma.

Sensitive Airways

When a person has asthma, their airways are always super-sensitive. Breathing in an irritant or allergen can cause an asthma attack. Even exercise, cold air, or emotional upsets can trigger an attack in some people. Different people have different triggers. Some are sensitive to smoke or chemicals. Others are more sensitive to allergens such as pollen.

Cold air can irritate a person's lungs and worsen asthma symptoms.

26

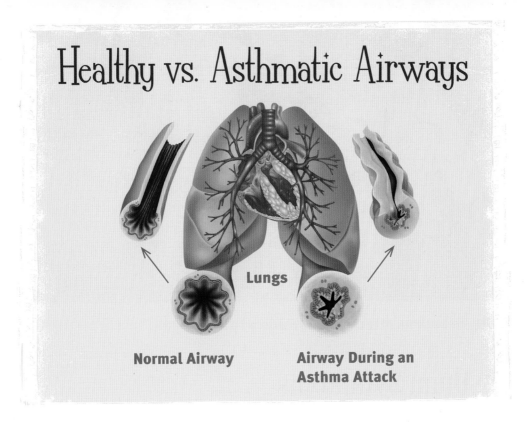

Healthy vs. Asthmatic Airways

Lungs

Normal Airway

Airway During an Asthma Attack

What Happens During an Asthma Attack?

When a person breathes in a triggering substance, tiny particles of the substance cause more irritation and swelling in the bronchial tubes. The muscles surrounding the tubes may tighten, narrowing the airways even further. The airways also produce lots of mucus, which clumps together and clogs the already-narrowed airways.

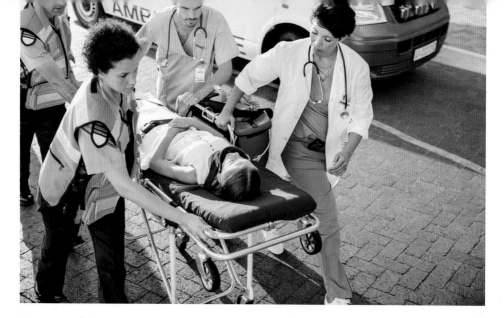
Severe asthma attacks require a trip to a hospital.

Asthma Symptoms

When a person has an asthma attack, breathing becomes very difficult. Usually, exhaling is more difficult than inhaling. Coughing, wheezing, and rapid breathing are common. The person sometimes feels a sense of panic as he or she gasps for air. The symptoms can usually be stopped quickly with an inhaler. However, if the attack is very bad, it may be necessary to call an ambulance.

Who Gets Asthma?

Asthma seems to run in families. If one parent has asthma, a person is three to six times more likely to develop it. If both parents have asthma, the person's chances rise even higher. Asthma often develops during childhood, and boys are almost twice as likely as girls to develop it at that age. People who have allergies are also more likely to develop the disease.

Asthma is not contagious. You cannot catch it from someone the way you would catch a cold.

Asthma, like allergies, is common in some families.

Other Risk Factors

Babies born too early are more likely to develop asthma. So are babies who are born through a surgical procedure called a Cesarean section. Having atopy (AT-uh-pee) also puts a person at risk for developing asthma. Atopy is a condition that causes extra sensitivity to allergens in the nose, skin, or lungs. Exposure to smoke and other pollution over time increases the risk of developing asthma. In adults, stress and obesity (being very overweight) are linked with higher rates of asthma.

Many places have banned smoking to protect the public's health.

In many people, asthma develops while they are still very young.

Different Types of Asthma

Asthma that develops in childhood is called child-onset asthma. It is a type of allergic asthma. Children who have a tendency toward asthma become very sensitive to allergens in their environment. Before long, those substances become triggers for asthma attacks. Asthma is the most common chronic disease in children. It affects about 7 million kids in the United States.

Fumes created through welding can lead to asthma.

People who develop asthma when they are 20 years of age or older have adult-onset asthma. Sometimes this asthma is related to the person's allergies, but not always. The nonallergic type is called intrinsic asthma. It can be triggered by stress, exercise, cold air, and other factors. Chemicals or other irritants in a person's workplace can also cause this type of asthma. It usually goes away when the person is not in contact with the irritating substances.

Nighttime Asthma

One of the strangest types of asthma is nighttime, or nocturnal, asthma. The usual cause is allergens such as dust mites or pet dander that are present in large amounts in the person's bedroom. Nocturnal asthma is hard to diagnose. A person may not even be aware of having symptoms, unless they wake him or her up during the night. And the symptoms never occur during daytime visits to the doctor!

A person's bed can contain a lot of pet dander, particularly if the pet sleeps on the bed.

Treating Asthma

Asthma is a chronic condition and cannot be cured. Asthma treatment focuses on two things. The first is long-term control of the disease, preventing flare-ups of asthma symptoms. The second is short-term relief, stopping symptoms when an asthma attack occurs. People who have asthma need to know all they can about both treatment methods. Neither one on its own is enough to keep someone healthy and safe.

Plastic tubes called spacers make it easier to use an inhaler.

Prevention Strategies

Most people with asthma take medicine every day to reduce inflammation. Such medicines are usually taken through an inhaler or **nebulizer**. These devices deliver a mist of medicine through the airways and into the lungs. If allergens trigger a person's asthma, a doctor might provide medicine to keep the patient's body from reacting to those substances. It is important to take medicines as instructed, even when feeling well. Long-term medications help prevent attacks from occurring.

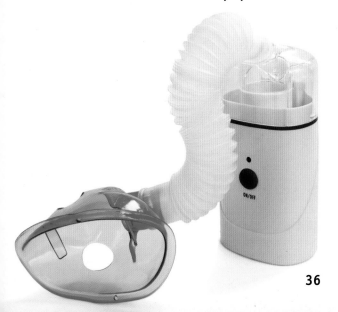

Nebulizers turn liquid medication into a vapor, which a patient breathes in through a mask.

Many people with asthma avoid using air fresheners, which irritate their lungs.

Avoiding Your Triggers

It is also important to avoid asthma triggers. This may mean keeping pets out of the bedroom or getting a fish instead of a dog or cat. It might mean staying indoors when there is a lot of pollen or air pollution. It could mean avoiding perfumes, air fresheners, and other irritants. By knowing and avoiding triggers, a person can have fewer asthma attacks—and the ones that do occur may be less serious.

A person with asthma should carry a rescue inhaler at all times, using it at the first sign of an asthma attack.

Rescue Strategies

An asthma attack may occur even with long-term treatment. This is when short-term medicines become necessary. A rescue inhaler can give quick relief by delivering a medicine that relaxes the tight muscles surrounding the airways. The inhaler doesn't reduce inflammation or stop the production of mucus. Because of this, a rescue inhaler cannot replace daily asthma medicine. A person needs to understand and use both to keep asthma under control.

Asthma on the Increase

Asthma rates have increased dramatically over the past few decades. Doctors once thought it was because our world was becoming "too clean." Technology has improved medicines and kept homes and people cleaner. But exposure to illnesses early in life teaches the body what is harmful and what is not. Doctors argue that this would prevent the body from overreacting to the wrong substances, as it does with asthma.

However, asthma is increasing even in countries with high rates of childhood disease. Now doctors wonder if it is due to a higher rate of obesity, which causes inflammation throughout the body. Another possibility is that people are not as active as they once were. This results in decreased lung strength. At this point, though, the real answer to why asthma is increasing is "We don't know!"

Many people have learned to manage their asthma and become successful athletes despite the illness.

Listening to your body and managing your asthma takes practice.

Asthma Action Plan

To keep asthma under control, a patient and doctor might fill out an asthma action plan. The plan includes medicines and doses, a list of triggers to avoid, and instructions on what to do if symptoms worsen. Plans are often divided into three zones: green, yellow, and red. In the green zone, a person has few or no symptoms. Yellow is a caution zone: symptoms are becoming worse. Red signals an emergency.

Using a Peak Flow Meter

A peak flow meter is a small device that measures the air moving in and out of the lungs. Many people with asthma regularly check their breathing with a meter. The first step is to measure their peak flow when they are feeling well and have no asthma symptoms.

That measurement is their "personal best." A drop in peak flow numbers can give an early warning that their asthma is worsening.

A peak flow meter is an easy way to track your asthma symptoms.

42

Living with asthma is easier with some preparation and the support of friends and family.

Living With Asthma

By following his asthma action plan and regularly checking in with the doctor, Kyle learned that having asthma doesn't have to be a big deal. He can exercise, play, and do pretty much everything his friends without asthma can do. If you have asthma, pay attention to your doctor's suggestions. You'll discover that living with asthma is easier than you may have thought. ★

Number of people around the world who suffer from asthma: More than 235 million

Number of Americans who suffer from asthma: 26 million

Number of children in the United States who suffer from asthma: Almost 7 million (about 1 in every 10 children)

Number of school days missed in the United States each year because of asthma: 13 million

Number of asthma-related emergency-room visits in the United States each year: 2.1 million

Percent of people with hay fever who also develop asthma: 25

Annual cost of asthma-related health care in the United States: $50 billion

Did you find the truth?

(F) There are no long-term treatments for asthma.

(T) Asthma can develop in adults.

Resources

Books

Dozor, Allen J., and Kate Kelly. *The Asthma and Allergy Action Plan for Kids: A Complete Program to Help Your Child Live a Full and Active Life*. New York: Simon & Schuster, 2004.

Silverstein, Alvin, Virginia Silverstein, and Laura Silverstein Nunn. *Handy Health Guide to Asthma*. Berkeley Heights, NJ: Enslow Publishers, 2013.

Visit this Scholastic Web site for more information on asthma:
★ www.factsfornow.scholastic.com
Enter the keyword **Asthma**

Important Words

allergens (AL-ur-jinz) — substances such as pollen or peanuts that trigger an unpleasant reaction

asthma (AZ-muh) — a lung disease that causes difficulty in breathing

infections (in-FEK-shuhnz) — illnesses caused by bacteria or viruses

inflammation (in-fluh-MAY-shuhn) — redness, swelling, heat, and pain, usually caused by an infection, injury, or allergic reaction

mucus (MYOO-kuhss) — a thick, slimy liquid that coats and protects the inside of a person's mouth, nose, throat, and other breathing passages

nebulizer (NEB-yuh-lye-zur) — a machine that turns liquid asthma medication into a fine mist that can be inhaled into the lungs

respiratory (RES-pur-uh-tor-ee) — having to do with the act or process of breathing in and breathing out

sinuses (SYE-nus-iz) — four hollow channels in the skull around the eyes and nose, all leading to the nose

symptoms (SIMP-tuhmz) — signs of an illness

Index

Page numbers in **bold** indicate illustrations.

About the Author

Ann O. Squire is a psychologist and an animal behaviorist. Before becoming a writer, she studied the behavior of rats, tropical fish in the Caribbean, and electric fish from central Africa. Her favorite part of being a writer is the chance to learn as much as she can about all sorts of topics. In addition to *Asthma* and books on other health topics, Dr. Squire has written about many different animals, from lemmings to leopards and cicadas to cheetahs. She lives in Long Island City, New York.